Discover Your Path to Leadership

Amber E. Williams

Dardon Books

ISBN-13: 978-0-9820973-1-1

Printed in the United States of America

Preface

My supervisor, the woman that interviewed me for the job, recommended me for hire, and championed me throughout the vetting process, walked onto my campus at the beginning of the school day during the first week of school. Her displeasure with what she saw from the front gate of the school to the front office was evident by her facial expression, but she wasn't the type of woman to leave things unsaid. She proceeded to tell me everything that was wrong in a frantic rant that, had it been a written paragraph, would not have contained any punctuation whatsoever. She demanded that I assemble my assistant principals immediately—it didn't matter what they were doing because this was mandatory and critical. The team assembled quickly and I sat at the conference table with them, unsure about what to do or say, if anything at all. My supervisor rekindled her rant, this time loaded with f-bombs and other profane words. I sat there as she demeaned our work on the campus and treated me like one of my assistant principals rather than the principal of the school. "This is f---ed up!" she shouted with emphasis, ripped a sheet of paper off the chart-sized Post-it pad, and began writing our get-better plan.

When I was in the third grade, I had a phenomenal teacher. She planted the seed in my heart to become a teacher. I remember a writing assignment that she gave us at the beginning of the school year. She took the class outside during the fall season and we had to write a paragraph describing a tree. The leaves were bright orange and red. During the winter season, she took us outside to write about the tree again. This time the leaves had fallen off and the tree looked cold and dead. We went outside one last time to write about the tree in the spring. The leaves had returned and were a vibrant green. The tree had come back to life! Somehow, through this writing process, our class bonded with this tree. We also ended the school year with writing samples that showed our parents our writing growth over the school year. There were so many things that my third-grade teacher did that, as an educator, I now recognize to be excellent teaching strategies. Even though I was just a little girl and didn't understand why my teacher taught us the way she did, I knew I wanted to be like her and do what she did when I grew up.

As I continued into middle school and high school, that seed grew and became rooted. I chose my university based on the notion that I wanted to be a teacher. When I entered college, I was exposed to a whole new world and for the first time began to doubt my commitment to becoming a teacher. After I graduated with my bachelor's degree in English, I applied for a teaching job at a charter school. They called me in for an interview and hired me right away. I was in awe that someone was going to entrust me with the education of young people! My first teaching job was a high school English position teaching recovered dropouts and students at risk of dropping out. They were a difficult bunch, but we loved each other, worked hard, and were successful as a team. My success over the next three years did not go unnoticed—I was asked to take on a leadership position at the school. I accepted and soon experienced success in my new leadership role. I also realized that I loved coaching others. Unfortunately, despite being at the height of its academic performance, the school was closed down for financial reasons and I found myself displaced. The area superintendent at the time was familiar with my work and she placed me at another charter school in a similar position. After spending only a year at that school, she asked me to open up a brand new charter high school. I was honored and overwhelmed! I completed that project and continued to progress in my career. I received my most challenging assignment yet—leading an underperforming traditional high school as principal. Never once during my high school or undergraduate education did I envision myself in campus leadership, much less a principal. How often do you hear children say, "I want to be a principal when I grow up!"? I found myself to be in an unexpected place--a place of learning and growth. It is through my journey in the field of education that I have discovered valuable keys to leadership and realized what it means to be a woman in leadership.

We as women have power. One of the reasons that most of us do not go as far as we can is because we are fearful. Fear contradicts power. When you know you have power, you act accordingly—you have confidence, assertiveness, and drive. When you are fearful, you have self-doubt, timidity, and lack of motivation. We were not created to be fearful, but to be powerful! The problem is that, even if we were to wake up every day believing that we are powerful, there are experiences that women have in life on a daily basis that chip away at the spirit of power and feeds the power of fear if we do not know how to deal with it. The beauty of sisterhood is that someone has been where you have been and someone has gone where you are going. Fear stems from the unknown and it can be extinguished when you know what's coming. Having a coach and a mentor can guide you along your path to success, help you to reduce your fear, and empower you to be the woman in leadership that you are designed to be. This book is meant to encourage you to start your journey of empowerment in leadership, but every woman's journey is unique, which is why you need a personal leadership coach to help you walk your individual path.

Chapter One

You don't know as much as you think you do?

I consider myself to be a life-long learner. At the time of my second principal position, I brought a wealth of experience to the table. I traditionally worked with at-risk youth in dropout recovery-type programs, so I professed to have had seen it all. I traveled the country to attend professional conferences, I read books and journal articles in my field, and I participated in professional development. With so much knowledge, how was it possible that I knew so little? Educators tend to do what I call "book shaming". It begins with, "Have you read such-and-such book?" and ends with a look of condemnation that you are not well-versed in the latest phase, fad, or trend in education and leadership. In the beginning, I would feel embarrassed and I would say a silent prayer of thanks to God that I had brown skin that didn't blush easily. I would rush to research the book, purchase it, and, after a brief perusal, put it on my shelf. But that's where the books stayed. I soon learned that just as quickly as a book was mentioned, it was replaced by the next best thing. That is not to say that there were not great things written in these books—it was that the people who read them had short attention spans and no intention of really applying anything that they read in a practical manner. Once I had that epiphany, I could no longer be book-shamed. When someone mentioned a new resource, I would reply, "I haven't read that one yet, but it sounds informative. Can you give me the name again and the author?" And just like that, they were validated and I didn't feel like an idiot. I kept the list of book titles and authors in my notebook and as time permitted, I researched them and gleaned what info I could from them.

One of my pet peeves is having something explained to me that I already understand. This is now called "mansplaining" but the truth is that men aren't the only ones who do this. When you are a young Black woman, there are many things that people assume that you don't know or aren't familiar with. I have uncomfortably sat in many conversations, patiently waiting for my colleague to finish explaining some term, policy, or program that I understood and probably had been using longer than them. In the beginning, I would interrupt them to profess my knowledge of whatever topic was being discussed. I found that my interruption did not sit well with them and so I began the practice of patiently enduring an explanation and finding an appropriate slot in the conversation to insert a comment that only a person familiar with the topic would be able to make. That was my personal victory. That's when I realized that Black, young, and woman were all terms that were synonymous with naive, dumb, and inexperienced. Those perceptions had nothing to do with the amount of knowledge and experience that I actually had. Assumptions were made about me upon my entry into a conference room. I knew I couldn't change stereotypes, but I could be an exception to whatever rule they applied to me and perhaps plant a seed of doubt in their mind about the know-how and knowledge of a young black woman in leadership. I read even more and I researched further the topics that were brought up in conversations. In meetings, my comments were informed and precise. Slowly but surely, my reputation became one of sharpness, wit, and intellect.

That strategy helped me to cope in the organization that I was in, but it did not entirely solve my problem. I also knew that I would not be with that organization for the rest of my life and I could encounter the same bias at the next job, the next job, and the next job. Unless your reputation is so grand that it precedes you everywhere you go, it helps to have some credentials behind your name for a variety of reasons. Credentials can help you get a job by setting you apart from other candidates. Credentials can also serve as vetting that you know what you say you know. If an acquaintance told me how to grow tulips in my backyard garden year round, I might be skeptical of the advice. However, if a gardener gave me the same information, I would be more likely to believe it and even apply it. Sometimes when my friends or family members get sick, I'll give them some advice to help them feel better and get over their cold more quickly. I'd venture to bet that they are skeptical about taking my advice (as I would be when they give it to me). Yet, they will go to the doctor and hear the exact same thing and follow the doctor's advice without hesitation. What's the difference? The advice given by a professional is taken more seriously. You want to put yourself in a position where you are viewed as a professional by those outside and within your field. In my field, credentials take the form of certifications and degrees. I do not recommend paying for licenses and certifications that do not benefit you in your field, but I do recommend being competitive in your field by being highly qualified and educated. I have earned multiple certifications over the years, which required an investment of my time and money. I also continued my college education, because the higher the career ladder I climbed, the more valuable the title of Dr. became, and I wanted that. Granted, you can be successful and have a great career without a degree or any kind, but I believe in going as far in your education as your circumstances will allow. When you educate yourself, you gain knowledge, prestige, and credibility in your field.

Chapter Two

There's more than one way to skin a cat (and your way is probably wrong).

In many of my leadership positions, even though I wasn't the top dog, I was often left to my own devices. That meant that I could complete tasks and projects however I saw fit, as long as I got it done. I earned this ability by producing quality work and performing well with little to no supervision. At a school where I was the assistant principal, the principal got particularly comfortable with my abilities and soon began "working from home" quite frequently. I was happy to "hold down the fort" while the principal was away. That meant that I could get things done without interruptions, without having to check in, and without having to make revisions based on someone else's opinion. I assumed that I would have this freedom as principal. In one principal position, I did have that freedom, and it was glorious! In another principal position, I did not have that freedom—in fact, I was micromanaged!

Imagine that you are a school leader and you have to address an issue on campus—let's use students' late arrival to school as an example. You spend hours devising a strategy to incentivize students to come on time and to track student data so that they can be held accountable. You present this strategy to your leadership team. You implement this strategy and it seems to be going well. Then, your boss comes on campus, asks about the plan, then tells you that you have to scrap your plan and implement her idea. What?! That happened to me (several times) and it was not a good feeling. All kinds of insubordinate thoughts ran through my head: *What if I told her that I would implement her plan but secretly wouldn't? What if I implemented her plan but sabotaged it so I can blame the failure on her?* I realized that my thoughts were immature and passive aggressive and that to buck up against my supervisor would cause more problems than what it was worth over a fairly minor issue. Even though no one really likes to be micromanaged, the real problem was my ego.

Through that experience as well as working with some of my peers, I learned to accept that there is more than one way to do things, and sometimes those other ways are just as good as or even better than my way. I learned to pick my battles. There were some plans that I wanted to implement my way because I would ultimately be held accountable for their success or failure. However, many times the issues were not critical and it didn't really matter how it got done or whose idea it was, it just needed to get done and be successful. Applying that concept to my relationship with a superior was difficult because I wanted to be top dog. I wanted to be the leader, with all the rights and responsibilities that accompanied the title. On the other hand, applying that concept to my subordinates was much easier and made me a revered leader because of it. I provided my team with the tools, knowledge, and support to devise their own plans to solve problems. I didn't shove my solutions down their throats and, even if their plan wasn't perfect, I gave them feedback and let them work out the kinks. They were better leaders because of it and a true sign of a leader is the ability to produce other leaders.

One of the key reasons that my change of perspective was effective is that I learned the arts of compromise, inclusion, and release. Compromise usually means that two people have reached an agreement in which they both have made concessions. In this context though, sometimes the other party is completely unaware that you are compromising! For example, I was planning a parent event at my school. I wanted to host the event on a Thursday night at 6:00 pm. My supervisor would not be able to make it at that time and asked if I could change the time to 7:00 pm. Keep in mind, this was my event, my supervisor was not required to come, nor could she mandate when my event was to be held. True compromise might have involved both of us conceding and agreeing upon a time in the middle, like 6:30 pm. In this instance, I compromised and planned the event for 7:00 pm—she didn't have to compromise at all. I had several reasons for making the decision. First, it wasn't that big of a deal. This wasn't an issue that I needed to fight over. In fact, I planned it at 6:00 pm more for the convenience of school staff, including myself, than for any other reason. My parents were supportive of the original event time, as well as the later time. The second reason for compromising was that it actually benefitted me for my supervisor to attend the event and stand in solidarity with me. She did not have to attend and I wanted to show appreciation for her effort to participate. Finally, compromising at that time could give me leverage at a later time when I would not want to compromise. It was better to show that I could be flexible in certain circumstances than to always seem uncompromising. Compromising does not mean you are weak. It means that you have evaluated the situation and determined that you do not have to stand hard and fast on your stance, but instead can be flexible. If you complete a project and someone requests that you change the presentation template, can you compromise? If you develop a plan and your colleague asks you to revise portions of it, can you compromise? If a customer asks you to tailor a standard product package for them, can you compromise? To determine whether or not you should compromise, think about why you do not want to compromise and the possible consequences of compromising. Often, we do not want to compromise because we are stubborn, want to do things our way, or feel disrespected or devalued when we are asked to change or adjust. If the consequences of compromising only include you getting your feelings hurt, then there is probably no reason to be inflexible. When my supervisor asked me to change the time of my parent meeting, if the change would have inconvenienced the parents, I would not have compromised. Likewise, if other people will be negatively affected by your decision to compromise, then it may not be the best idea. However, if the benefits of compromising outweigh the consequences, then try being more flexible.

Another strategy for effectively working with supervisors and teams is the art of inclusion. Ideas and plans that are created by a lone individual in seclusion are more likely to be criticized and knocked down. This is because most plans require other individuals to be involved, whether they are implementing the plan or simply have to provide their stamp of approval. When these stakeholders do not get a say-so in the plan, they do not have buy-in and often are resentful of having someone else's idea shoved down their throat. No matter how good a plan may be, it can be ill-received if no one else had an opportunity to provide their input. Inclusion becomes an art because, if you do it effectively, you will still have autonomy over your project and idea, but others will feel part of the process. Begin your project by asking for input. Ask team members for their thoughts or opinions about the issue or problem you are addressing with your project. You may be surprised that, as the leader, your perspective of a problem differs from your team's perspective. For example, I surveyed the teachers on campus and discovered that they wanted more opportunities to provide feedback about the operations of the campus. I initially had grandiose plans of forming focus groups and advisory boards of teachers to discuss teaching and learning on campus. However, before I acted on that idea, I asked a few teachers about the concern. It turned out that what I was planning was more than what they needed. They simply wanted a simple and efficient way of communicating their concerns to me so that they could be addressed. Instead of occupying everyone's time with unnecessary meetings, I placed a suggestion box in the teachers' lounge. Some of the concerns had to do with teaching and learning, but many of their concerns were about the day-to-day functionality of the campus and staff that kept them from doing their job effectively. I acknowledged the concerns that were submitted in the suggestion box and also detailed the remedy (such as adding a second microwave to the teacher's lounge on the second floor).

Another way to facilitate inclusion is to brief supervisors or peers about plans or ideas before you have completed the final version. This gives them the opportunity to provide feedback before you are done which cuts down on the frustration that occurs when you have to revise what you considered a finished project. This type of inclusion can be very informal. I would tell my supervisor that I wanted to "run an idea by her". This let her know what I was thinking about doing and gave her the opportunity to share her thoughts or parameters before I invested too much time in the project. People tend to be less critical when it's their work too. When you include others in the planning process, they are much more likely to feel a sense of "we" rather than "I" and "you".

Lastly, there is the art of release. Also known as the art of letting go, this is probably the hardest strategy to implement for some. If you are a leader, then you have probably achieved your role or title because you get things done and are good at what you do. However, the higher up you go, the more you have to work through others. The art of letting go is about letting others take over an idea, task, or project without your involvement. You may have a great idea in your head or a solid plan that is sure to work. Let it go. Let one of your team members take it on and give them the space and opportunity to do it without you inserting your ideas. Your supervisor may want you to do something a certain way, perhaps almost the opposite of the way you were thinking about doing it. Let it go. Just do it their way.

Chapter Three

Action takes planning, but planning isn't better than action.

I am a doer. I have a reputation for getting things done, both professionally and in my personal life. Never in my career had I encountered the necessity for so much planning! Plans had to be discussed, written, discussed again, revised, printed and emailed, and presented. By the time the process was complete, the plans were outdated! Written plans were how you proved to someone who was not physically present that you were on the ball and had things handled. I became a great plan writer to keep the monkeys off my back.

Leadership takes balance. My "doing" nature had to be toned down—I could not be the Lone Ranger and do, do, do without letting anyone know what was going on or why. I also could not be swayed to the other extreme and be so bogged down by planning that nothing ever got done. I became skilled at action planning. Every issue was evaluated to find its root cause. Every root cause was addressed with an action plan. Tasks on the action plan were delegated and assigned. There was accountability. There was follow up. There were results! I found a way to appease those who demanded plans and to be productive at the same time.

Planning is a necessary part of the leadership role. The act of planning forces you to analyze the problem or goal and to systematically address it. Planning also helps to detail out the specifics of the action to be taken so that others can be brought on board for implementation. Planning is vital, whether a business has one employee or one thousand. However, I have witnessed many leaders spend so much time on planning that they never acted or ran out of time to act when issues were time sensitive. I have witnessed leaders who could draft eloquent plans, but their execution was horrible. I have also witnessed leaders who did not dedicate enough time to drafting clear plans so the execution was terrible because no one knew what to do. An effective leader understands that planning is part of the process and that planning should be done effectively and in a timely manner. No one wants to work for a leader that is always flying by the seat of their pants. Employees and team members feel reassured by plans, systems, and processes that are efficient and effective.

Chapter Four

You're only as good as your last miracle.

My first official leadership role was as a department chair. My supervisor at the time was experiencing some turmoil in his position. I always find a way to learn from all of my bosses, good or bad, and even in all his franticness, this boss taught me something. He told me, "You're only as good as your last miracle." Never had more prophetic words been spoken in the world of urban education. He was in the process of experiencing an expired miracle and was desperate to find another. He didn't and he was soon let go.

Miracles are very public displays. They are manifestations of your leadership, your expertise, and your success. Maybe your miracle is stellar sales for the quarter, closing on the most properties, securing a high-dollar contract, or something of the sort. Many of my miracles got me promotions, the next job, and accolades. However, while you are riding the wave of one miracle, you must be thinking about how you are going to produce the next one. Tides turn quickly and the same people that were singing your praises last month could be pointing the finger at you next month. Miracles keep your reputation positive. They establish your brand. They even provide a bit of forgiveness when you screw up. A tragic mistake is to ride the wave of a miracle too long and not realize that it's expiring. You may then find yourself desperately trying to produce a miracle that won't happen soon enough.

You cannot rest on your laurels. You have to continue to out-do yourself and reinvent yourself time and again.

How do you create a miracle? Identify a goal for your department or organization that would be publicly praised if it were accomplished. This goal might be related to an area that the company has been lacking in for a while with no hope of improving. The goal also must be able to be measured in a timely manner. Waiting on end-of-year results could delay your miracle. Perhaps sales in a certain department are down or student attendance is low. Perhaps there is an opportunity for your department to work on a community project. An ideal focus area would garner media attention, the attention of the community, the attention of senior-level employees of the organization, or some similar type of attention. Once you identify the goal, be laser-focused on achieving it. You may need to use unconventional methods to get it done and it may require longer, harder work hours in addition to your normal duties and responsibilities. It's not important that everyone knows you are working on the goal, but it is very important that you get the credit for achieving it. This is not the time to be shy, humble, or modest!

Chapter Five

Getting results doesn't always make you a good

leader.

Just because a leader gets good results doesn't mean that they are a good leader. In one of my leadership positions, the leaders that were over me were recently promoted to this new title that gave them the authority to supervise other principals, including me. These leaders got these jobs by doing their job well—for one or two years. This practice of quick promotion based on results bred leaders who would do ANYTHING to get results so they could achieve the next title and a six-figure salary. This strategy worked because results didn't have to be sustainable, they only had to be impressive for a year or two. When the leadership changed, many of the schools that these former principals led went through turmoil and reduced performance.

Unfortunately, leaders like those can appear successful because there are some bad leadership traits that can produce good results in the short term. Leaders like these can be demeaning to employees. They may belittle employees in front of others, reprimand publicly, or throw tantrums when informed of bad news or poor performance. These types of behaviors instill fear in employees. Fearful employees do their job because they are afraid of what will happen if they don't. However, fearful employees also plot your demise and sabotage plans while you're not looking. Other poor leadership traits include lying, manipulating, threatening, bribing, cheating (and the list could go on and on). In the long run, leaders like these can face the repercussions of their behavior, unless they are quickly promoted or leave to another job.

I led differently because I didn't want the same promotion that they wanted. My end goal was to do my job well and to create systemic change where I was. I wasn't going to "do my time" and leave, as some referred to it. I didn't want to be known as a villain, I wanted to be known as a great leader. I listened to employees, valued their opinions, and included them in the decision-making process. I didn't bend rules. I was forthcoming with information. I thought about one of my former principals yelling at employees using expletives and being unmoved by tears. I didn't want to be that kind of a leader, even if it meant that it would take me longer to get the results that I was looking for. As one of my colleagues expressed, "I refused to sell my soul". Taking the high road sometimes takes longer, but when you do, you reap positive rewards like employee loyalty, dedication, and work ethic, and well-operating systems. For me, the end does not justify the means and there are some things that are more important than the bottom line.

Chapter Six

Sometimes it's just not about you.

I used to think that some people were out to get me. They were staying up late at night plotting my demise and conspiring with the people around me. I was paranoid and probably a bit egotistical to think that I was worth all that trouble. I learned that some people have ulterior motives for doing the things that they do and it's not necessarily about you. You may be a means to an end or a pawn in a scheme, but it's not always about YOU. In fact, many of the leaders that I have described thus far are narcissistic—too narcissistic to be that focused on someone else. Narcissistic leaders are focused on themselves and you may be in the way.

Narcissistic leaders use the words "I" and "me" more often than "we" or "us". They often lack emotion and are unsympathetic towards others' displays of emotion. On the other hand, they will fake emotions to manipulate others. Narcissistic leaders rarely support any idea or project that will not benefit them in some way. They forget what you told them and don't like to admit fault.

So if it's not about you, then what is it about? As a leader, it's your job to discover what motivates people. Everyone is motivated by something, including your boss. Some are motivated by money—they want a promotion because of the higher salary, they want the bonus, or the high commission checks. Others are motivated by recognition—they want the employee of the month award, a public celebration of a milestone or accomplishment, or a plaque to go on a wall. Then there are others who are motivated by power—they want the promotion because of the rank and status, they want to tell people what to do, or they want the authority to take the lead on a project. There are other motivators, but the key is to find out what drives each person that you work with. Once you realize what their motivator is, it makes it easier to work with that person. I discovered that one of my bosses was motivated by recognition; she wanted to be shouted out publicly. I told her, "I can make you look good if you let me do my job." I prioritized some projects that would get her quick (and public) wins. She was happy.

You just can't take everything personally. You have to grow a thicker skin and realize that sometimes people are just trying to get what they want, even if it means that they have to go around you, over you, or through you to get it. Just like you need to discern the motivations of others, you need to figure out what motivates you. That's important because if you are not getting your needs met, you may find yourself behaving like other narcissistic leaders and stopping at nothing to obtain what motivates you. My motivation is private recognition. I will go above and beyond for a personally expressed "well done" or "good job". Knowing my motivation helped me to identify and acknowledge my frustration when I did not have my needs met as a leader. Knowing yourself as a leader is just as important as knowing who you're leading and who you're being led by.

Chapter Seven

There is power in mentoring and coaching.

I have always said that I stand on the shoulders of giants. I also always say that I was pulled into leadership. I would not have had the success that I have had without the wisdom and guidance of my mentors and coaches. There is a difference between a mentor and a coach. A mentor is usually a person who has been down the career path that you are beginning. They may offer advice, act as a sounding board as you work through ideas or issues, and offer suggestions for action. A coach is different from a mentor in that they strategically help you with skill-building to become more effective in your current role. Finding a mentor can happen by chance. Establishing a coaching relationship is deliberate.

My first coach was provided to me through my school. I was a classroom teacher and testing scores needed to increase in every grade level and every subject. Before the coach came in, I was using good teaching strategies, but I wasn't preparing students for what they needed to know on the state test. When I was hired, I was thrown into the classroom with very little support and even fewer resources. I was a pull-yourself-up-by-your-own-bootstraps kind of teacher so I made great things happen anyway. After so long of doing things on my own and my way, I did not like the idea of someone else coming in trying to tell me how to do my job. I was resentful that they sent this coach into my classroom and I gave her a bit of resistance. She persevered and was able to show me my strengths along with my weaknesses and what I could do to improve them. She showed me some effective techniques for preparing my students for the standardized test. As I began to see results from her coaching, I soaked up every little piece of advice that she could provide. School administration took notice and soon I was preparing the entire student body for the state test in large groups assembled in the cafeteria. That year, test scores soared and I had my first miracle—all thanks to my coach.

My coach stuck with me through my next few positions as I transitioned into leadership. I found that the nature of our relationship began to change. She became more of a mentor than a coach because the strategic skill-building had ceased. She now offered tidbits of advice here and there and was always a phone call away when I had a question. I realized that I needed a new coach. I did not find another true coach until years later, even though I had many mentors in the interim. Once again, my coach was assigned to me, not self-selected. The difference this time was that I now understood the power of the coach and I was ready to forge a positive relationship with this woman. She taught me a lot and coached me through some difficult situations. I owe much of my later success to her.

Mentoring is a great development tool for anyone, whether you are already in leadership or desire to be. Mentoring helps you to refine your career vision and goals, builds you up professionally, and adds to your professional network. However, coaching is a much more powerful tool that develops effective leaders. If you have not been provided an opportunity to be coached, search for that opportunity yourself. The best training in leadership is one-on-one and if you want to be on the fast track to successful leadership, this is a step that you cannot skip. Invest in yourself and your future in leadership by getting a coach.

Chapter Eight

You are enough.

I was, am, and always will be an overachiever. I am degreed and certified. I have years of experience in my field. I have received many accolades in my career. My mentors reaffirmed my strengths and qualifications. My coaches helped me to turn my weaknesses into strengths. I have data to show my efficacy. Yet, with every position that I obtained, in the back of my mind I would think, *"Why would they want me? Can I really do this?"* I would doubt myself—I believed that I was sorely lacking in some key area and my being placed in a leadership position was a fluke. Every time that something went wrong, instead of believing that it was an unforeseeable issue or a result of human error, I blamed myself and believed that I wasn't good enough to do the job. Any criticism that I received was an indication that I wasn't good enough and they wanted someone else.

Some might say that I was a victim of low self-esteem. I can assure you that that was not the case. My professional career is one of the aspects of my life where I am the most confident in my abilities. I had self-doubt because I was a walking trifecta of discrimination. I was a young, black woman in leadership. I moved quickly up the career ladder so I was a noticeably young leader. Even as I grew older, my good genes were both a blessing and a curse. People assumed that I didn't have experience or knowledge in some areas or just couldn't relate to things that happened years ago because I looked younger than I was. There were some days that I longed for a few gray hairs and wrinkles (I'm glad those prayers were not answered!). The majority of teachers are women, yet somehow leadership in education is dominated by males. I believe that women are breaking glass ceilings in education, but there are still only a few female superintendents and the women that hold these positions are paid significantly less. As a woman, I experienced "microaggressions" from my male colleagues—little discriminatory remarks in relation to my gender. There was pressure regarding my appearance that men didn't have to conform to. If I had a bad hair day, I had a self-doubt day. To complete the triad of discrimination, add the racial component. There was a pervasive belief and culture that black leaders only understood urban education and that their knowledge and expertise did not translate over to other demographics and cultures. This belief created dead-end career tracks for Blacks in educational leadership. I didn't wake up in the morning doubting my abilities, nor did the self-doubt fall upon me as I fought traffic on the way to work. Self-doubt occurred when I came into contact with people who treated me as less-than.

As a leader, there are many ways that you can overcome self-doubt. First, you cannot remain isolated. You do not have to be a "man on an island". Seek out other leaders that you can vent to, commiserate with, and exchange encouraging words with. You will realize that your situations and feelings are not unique and that despite your flaws or weaknesses, you have what it takes to do your job well. Second, find an accountability partner. Self-doubt can come from our desire to grow and better ourselves. As you set goals to improve yourself and your work, communicate these goals to your accountability partner. They should check on your progress toward your goals and encourage you to keep going. Lastly, the words we speak to ourselves are powerful. Our self-talk is usually what feeds our self-doubt. I believe in reciting positive aspirations or mantras to change my pattern of thinking. One of my favorites that I use often is "I am enough".

Reflection

I've learned innumerable lessons throughout my journey of leadership. Some of those lessons I have learned by watching others and some I have learned the hard way. As a lifelong learner, I know that I have many more lessons to learn before my time is done. Some of my key takeaways from my experiences are not about how to do my job, but about me.

1. Be a learner.
2. You are not the sole producer of solutions.
3. Be an action planner.
4. Be a miracle worker.
5. Be famous, not infamous.
6. It's not about you.
7. Find a coach.
8. You are enough.

In leadership, you must know who you are or someone is going to decide for you. You are always going to be too much or not enough of something as a woman in leadership. It's for you to decide what about yourself you are happy with and what you are willing to change. What are your values? What parts of your heritage do you take pride in? If you don't know, you will find yourself subject to the opinions and feedback from others—what you should wear, how you should style your hair, how you should balance being a mother and a leader, how you celebrate holidays. The list goes on and on. If you don't want someone else to step in and tell you what to value or devalue, figure it out for yourself and stand by it unapologetically.

I am known to be fierce and outspoken (or feisty by those who try to demean me). There are some things that, due to ethics, morals, or my personal philosophy, I refuse to back down on. When I received pushback from my superior regarding a decision that I made that I wouldn't back down on, she asked me in frustration, "Are you willing to die on the stake for this?" Without hesitation, I replied, "Yes!" In my industry, I believe it is my moral and ethical responsibility to do right by kids. To do that, there are some decisions that I make that, come hell or high water, I'm sticking to because I know it's the right thing to do. Dying on the stake could mean a reprimand or even a loss of a job, but it means that you didn't compromise. No matter how irreverent you believe the saying to be, you have to know what you are willing to die on the stake over.

Leadership is a lonely job. It is also probably very far removed from the job you loved that brought you into the industry. I started out as a teacher. I love teaching, I love learning, and I love kids. A principal can easily spend an entire school day on campus without having a meaningful interaction inside of a classroom. I wasn't that kind of principal. Staying away from the classroom made me lose sight of why I was doing what I was doing and I would get lost in the morass of school bureaucracy. I prioritized visiting classrooms and interacting with teachers and students. I had a cafeteria duty schedule so that I could be near the students. If I got stressed out, I would go tutor kids. That's where my passion was. Passion is always likened to a burning fire and it truly is like one. You have to feed it to keep it burning and it is always at risk of being extinguished. Know your passion and fuel it because, if you don't, both you and your passion will burn out.

One of my favorite poems is Robert Frost's "The Road Not Taken". It begins "Two roads diverged in a yellow wood and sorry I could not travel both". As I have taken many diverging pathways throughout my career, I often wondered, *What if I had made this choice or that choice instead?* What I have found is that the path is yours and yours alone—it will not be exactly like someone else's, nor should it be. However, unlike the traveler in Frost's poem, you do not have to walk the path alone. There is a large army of women—sisters, mentors, and coaches—who stand ready to walk beside you every step of the way. All you have to do is reach out and say that you are ready!

TAKE ACTION!

Complete these activities to help you reflect on your aspirations and practice as a leader and to help guide your movement forward.

Activity 1: Understand the emotions that sabotage your leadership abilities.

We allow people to make us feel a certain way. Guilt, shame, and embarrassment are just as much a reflection of how we feel about ourselves as they are a reflection of how others perceive us. What are some things that people have said or done to you that have made you feel guilty, ashamed, or embarrassed? How do you think you can reframe your thinking to eliminate those feelings? (Examples may include a lack of education, shamed by a family member, marital status, financial status, etc.)

Activity 2: As a leader, you must be a continuous learner.

Identify 5 books that are influential in your field or applicable to your industry. Purchase them and begin reading. Identify a training course or conference that you can attend that will help you learn and network.

Activity 3:   How important are credentials to you?

Have you considered going back to school?   Why or why not?   If you went back to school, what would your goal be?   What school would you attend?   Research what it would require for you to go back to school this year.   Remember that continuing education does not always mean pursuing a degree—you can earn a new certification or endorsement or simply acquire a new skill.

Activity 4: Know when to compromise and when to stand your ground.

Reflect on a time when you could have compromised but you did not. What were your reasons for not compromising? What was the result? Reflect on a time when you compromised and you should not have. Why did you regret compromising?

Activity 5: Change your self-talk.

Write three affirmations or mantras that can help change your self-talk and eliminate your self-doubt.

Activity 6: Reflect on your practice.

What have you learned from your experiences as a

leader or aspiring leader?   How have these lessons

impacted how you operate?

ABOUT THE AUTHOR

My name is Amber E. Williams and I am an education consultant and leadership coach. I have over 14 years of experience in education in both public and private schools. I have founded a charter school and created a nonprofit organization to help high school dropouts. I have also spoken at conferences and other events and provided training for educators. Currently, I am operating Williams Education Consulting and developing a new leadership coaching model for school leaders. My work includes coaching current and aspiring leaders in a variety of fields, providing training to educators, and supporting aspiring entrepreneurs.

I count myself as fortunate that I have had powerful and successful women to speak into my life and help to shape me into the leader that I have become.

One of those women was my mother, who passed away several years ago. To honor her legacy, I founded the Stepping Stone Scholarship to assist high school graduates to attend community college. It is my turn to pay it forward and be a positive influence on the leaders of tomorrow.

My goal as a leadership coach is to grow leaders to realize their full potential, to succeed in their current position, and to ready themselves for their future leadership positions. I specialize in transformational leadership—I provide one-on-one coaching that changes the lives of leaders and of the people that they serve. I offer targeted assistance to build upon strengths and to reduce weaknesses. I provide practical strategies to improve time management and increase efficiency. My services are available in person, by video conference, and by telephone. I am also available to speak at events on topics relating to leadership, entrepreneurship, and public education.

awilliams@amberewilliams.com

www.amberewilliams.com

http://amberewilliams.com/leadership-tips

Twitter: @amberonthemove

www.facebook.com/amberewilliams